This book belongs to:
_____

Look it's not difficult you just write your name along the line and, no, I haven't got a spare pen.

Welcome to Wheelie's World

Here's an exciting game for you and all your your friends

Well just you then, nevermind the friends. You'd like to but you're not sure you've got the time. You want to check your phone first. Alright, go ahead, perhaps it's something REALLY important. Look I shouldn't start this thing if your mind's not really on it. Another time then, OK leave it for now.

30 Go to see Wheelie Bag at Crazy Homies but cannot remember anything after 9.30. Nevermind you just hang out in this corner of the game as long as you want…

Sneak back into the game down here.

TEQUILA TOM

29

28 Find a box of Doctor Bird singles and give them straight to Deejay Wheelie Bag. Advance 10 spaces, in fact go anywhere you want. Cheers

SCAREY MARY

27 Do Wheelie's Quiz at the Spread Eagle and use www.quizanswers.com on your phone to defeat Phil's Mates. Win a prize but forever after your life is tinged with remorse and regret.

26

21

22 Find some bouncing light-up eyeballs in the Dalston Pound Shop, buy only one when you should have bought the whole box. Miss a go, but hang on maybe it's not too late to go back for the box, you do and it's gone. Now what did I tell you.

23

24 Win first prize in a beauty contest. Spend the proceeds at Intoxica Records. Miss a day but don't regret it.

25

20

19

18 Enjoy a relaxing mug of Bournevita malted milk drink. Realise you are in the wrong board game and go to sleep.

ZOMBIE BRIDE

17 Mess around with one of Vince Ray's graphics lose your life!

16

15 Doze off on the 236 bus and wake up in Hackney Wick. That's punishment enough. Move on 1 square.

14

Oooh er…

MISS REAPER

9 Find an old Dansette abandoned in the road, take it home, get it repaired and buy it a new stylus. ADVANCE 6 squares.

JOHNNY VOODOO

10 Get a proper job, stop behaving badly, buy an iPod. Hmmm this is serious you'd better leave the game.

11

12 You change the colour of Liam and Jo's rabbit to bright blue using temporary food dye. Now that's quite funny. Go on do it again. Does it work with green? Nevermind the game, what about orange and this stuff that glows in the dark…

13

8

7

6

5 WHAT! You forgot to go to Wheelie's Show. Start over again. Next time remember it's the first Wednesday of every month.

4

3 Go for a drink with everyone at Sounds That Swing. Lose a week.

2

1 Find a £1. Go straight to Dalston.

Throw up to START

Mr. DEAD LUCKY

CONTENTS

In the beginning: June 1999

Forward

Welcome to the first ever Wheelie Bag Annual

The Wheelie Bag is a customised sound system for people who like their music so much they want to rush off immediately and play it to their friends. Out the door, down the pub, plug in and go. This 'artwork' really works! Individually commissioned and themed, combining appearance with performance in a slice of pure music culture, the Wheelie Bag is assured a unique place in the history of entertainment.

(Come on Wheelie, knock it on the head, don't forget you're leaving at 10pm).

So here's to all the Wheelie Bag owners, and to the loyal and supportive audiences over the years. To event and festival organisers who have helped the Wheelie make its way across Europe and beyond. To Chris and her words of wisdom. To the Pound Shop owners of Dalston…

(He's off again, I don't believe it).

To these people and more this book is dedicated.

There, I've finished now.

Sorry it went on a bit.

I just wanted to say thanks, that's all.

Anyway cheers,

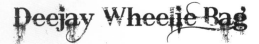

The early suitcase Wheelie Bags came in all shapes and sizes. Here's one that made it to 'The Wild Weekend' in Spain, I think in October 2000.

They tended to be cumbersome, heavy and unreliable.

'Hmmm... something's not quite working here...'

(Would that be to do with the braces, Wheelie, or the waistline?)

Wheelin' 'n' Rockin'
Part One

PRE-ROAMIN' TIMES

How to ruin a perfectly good suitcase

In pre-Roamin' times Wheelie Bags did not have any wheels! Somewhere around June 1999 the first Wheelie Bag came in a wooden fruit box. It used a battery powered record player with an additional car radio amplifier, a mic and a small mixer. It needed to be transported in the top box of a moped.

A pub outing in a double decker bus for a day at the races marked the first opportunity for a trial run.

'LESS IS MORE WHEELIE!'

It worked (badly) for hours! Most of the audience crammed onto the lower deck to get away from the noise but the owner of this fruit box juke box was undeterred. Flushed with success and tinned lagers he set about planning his next move, an uninvited 'pop-up' gig in Clerkenwell.

Thus did it come to pass that a few days before Christmas The Three Kings was blessed by the presence of the battery powered, banana panier, Wheelie Bag, with added revolving Barbies.

By no means a run-away success, (often was heard the comment 'less is more') its creator remained convinced that he was on to something. A better system could be built from scratch and a converted suitcase was the way to do it.

Plan B

The Wheelie Bag prototype makes its first appearance. Note the absence of wheels! I've still got those braces but seem to have lost some of the hair. Picture circa June 1999.

An imminent trip to Greece where it was booked to play at a birthday party was celebrated a couple of nights before in the usual style at The Three Kings (where else!).

The pre booking celebration proved a little premature as the entire construction fell apart in baggage reclaim at Athens airport.

Wheelin' 'n' Rockin'

Part Two

ROAMIN' TIMES

The Shopping Trolley Sound Systems

By 2001 it became apparent that there was so little left of an original suitcase by the time it had been modified that its choice for adaptation was not such a good idea. What else has wheels? The use of a shopping trolley seemed a logical next step. With the addition of some MDF wooden board, the building of the first Wheelie Bag commenced – with wheels! It consisted of a box to house an amplifier (from the wonderful Henry's Audio), a small deck, some records and speaker. In order for the machine to travel with its owner by bus its overall size was determined not only by the trolley in which it would sit but by the dimensions of the Routemaster luggage hold into which it could, on occasion, be shoved.

'The Enterprise', Red Lion Street.

In addition to playing records Wheelie Bag#1 included the ability to mount an occasional circular flight by a battery powered spaceman suspended in the front of the speaker. 'Rocket man,' (the precursor to The Wheelettes), seldom worked but fortunately the Wheelie Bag did and ensured a regular Wednesday night booking thereafter.

Another machine was soon underway for an artist and DJ in Norwich. This 'first commission' was swopped for a painting.

An era of building MDF boxes in modified shopping trolleys had begun and was to last about three years.

The cramped beginnings of the Wheelie workshop, underneath the spare bed. Plenty of room in the corduroy trousers though.

To everyone's surprise the first Wheelie Bag turned out ok, in an odd kind of way. It landed its owner his first booking at 'The Enterprise' pub in Red Lion Street.

Thank you Sara.

DJ Wheelitzer (Norwich)

Liam Watson (Toe Rag Studios) and a valve themed machine that I named DJ Marconi

Debbie with her rock chick system entitled DJ Debbie Does. The revolving heart at
the front was my idea, the burning deck... er... not mine.

Noah and Jono and their Trolley Troubadour Trophy winning machine — DJ Flat Dogs.
By the looks of it the dogs have won their own trophy.

Henry and Tim make up the CD playing, fashion conscious and horse themed Wheelie Bag posse known as The Caballo.

Maggi, also known as The Phatt Controller, with her James Brown referenced machine DJ Night Train.

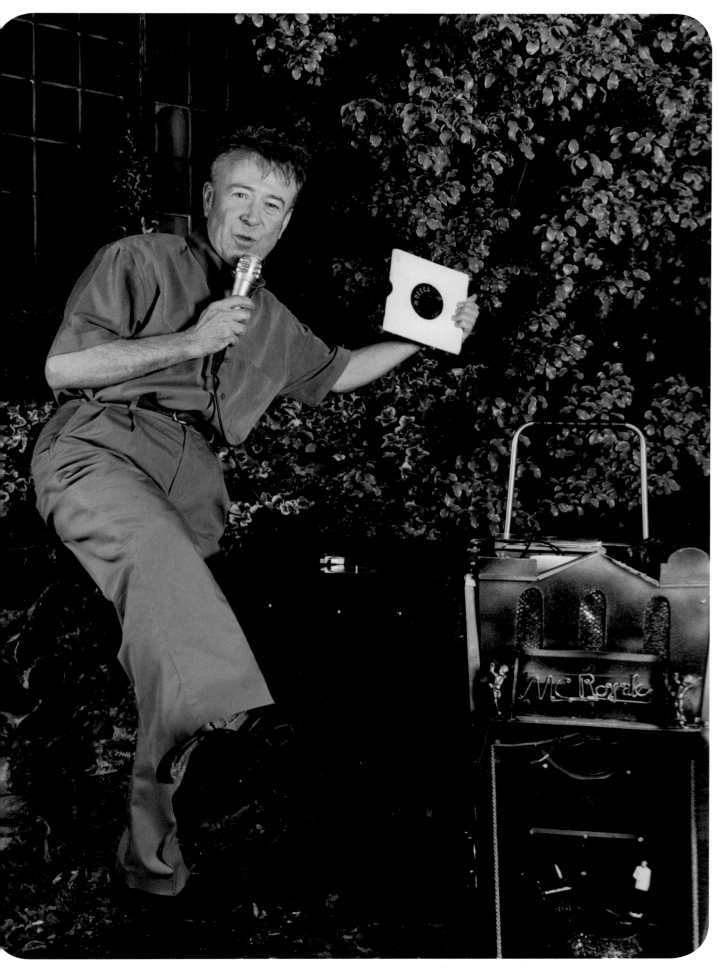

One time alternative Cabaret host and performer Ian, with a machine vaguely referenced to The Hackney Empire, DJ MC Royale.

DJ Wheelitzer: Norwich resident and artist Jon with his second machine. The wheels and glitter ball of an earlier version failed to survive the cobbled streets!

This machine, that I named DJ Veneer, continues to provide the sounds for Ben's long running club 'The Stag' down in the heart of Soho.

A contemplative Deejay Wheelie Bag on something like the third machine complete with one of the Wheelettes.

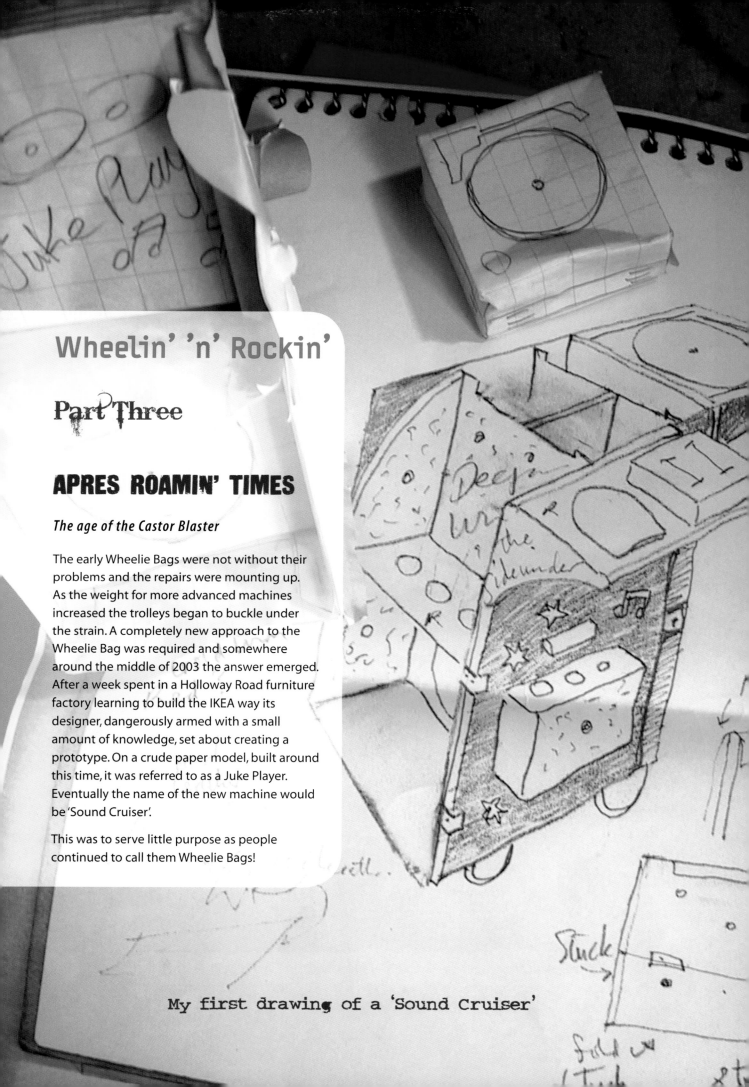

Wheelin' 'n' Rockin'

Part Three

APRES ROAMIN' TIMES

The age of the Castor Blaster

The early Wheelie Bags were not without their problems and the repairs were mounting up. As the weight for more advanced machines increased the trolleys began to buckle under the strain. A completely new approach to the Wheelie Bag was required and somewhere around the middle of 2003 the answer emerged. After a week spent in a Holloway Road furniture factory learning to build the IKEA way its designer, dangerously armed with a small amount of knowledge, set about creating a prototype. On a crude paper model, built around this time, it was referred to as a Juke Player. Eventually the name of the new machine would be 'Sound Cruiser'.

This was to serve little purpose as people continued to call them Wheelie Bags!

My first drawing of a 'Sound Cruiser'

The building method could no longer be based on wooden board. The small studio in which Wheelie Bags were built was also used to store records, it had already been invaded too many times by layers of wood dust. MDF, plywood, or any other wood, was, in any case, proving too heavy. The 'Sound Cruiser' would be made from 10mm, twin wall, polycarbonate. This versatile material is virtually unheard of outside the roofing business but it would revolutionise the making of a Wheelie Bag.

From now on the new style machines could be decorated using coloured adhesive vinyl, ideally suited to the smooth plastic surface which also allowed the very effective use of fluorescent and LED lights. Gone the shopping trolley and (to some people's dismay) the separate amplifier. Each Wheelie now had its own castor wheels and used an 'active' speaker.

THE FIRST 'SOUND CRUISER' WHEELIE BAG APPEARED IN 2004

The 'Sound Cruiser' was bigger than its predecessor, but so far as transport was concerned, larger buses had by now also replaced the Routemaster. It was lighter, louder and could be wheeled more easily. But the real significance of the new machine was the ease by which it could be customised to suit the growing variety of themes and ideas that future owners were coming up with. 'Commissioning' a Wheelie Bag was to become a key feature and marked the beginning of regular machine building from that point on until the present.

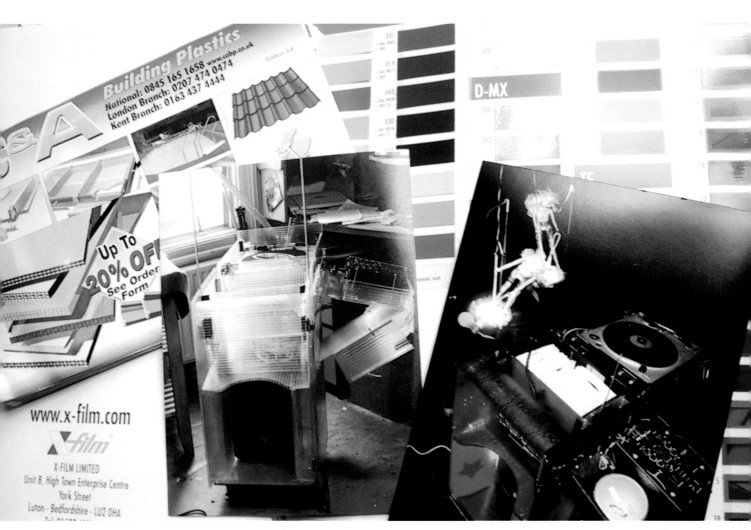

The first Polycarbonate Wheelie Bag construction takes shape in the studio with a final covered version completed with lights, coloured vinyls, snake skin effect fabric and, of course, the Wheelettes.

The new Wheelie Bag was a simple construction but had plenty of surface area to incorporate design or theme ideas as required.

Closed up it was roughly the size of a large suitcase and weighing in at around 25 kilos could even accompany its owner on a flight abroad. Opening up and preparing to play took a matter of a few minutes. Each machine came with a turntable, a mixer for the use of CD/iPod/MP3 player or any other format, a mic and an 'active' PA speaker. The rest of the design, colour, theme, DJ name and logo was up to the new owner.

An animated Gene Autry appears from behind a rock in this Western themed, cow hide lined machine for a clothing shop in Sweden. Its two positions allowed an upright mode for the shop window and a DJ mode for later in the evening.

GAZ'S ROCKIN BLUES

DJ GAZ MAYAL
Features: Gaz's Rockin
Blues graphics
Revolving 'Ska Barbies'.
Off road wheels.

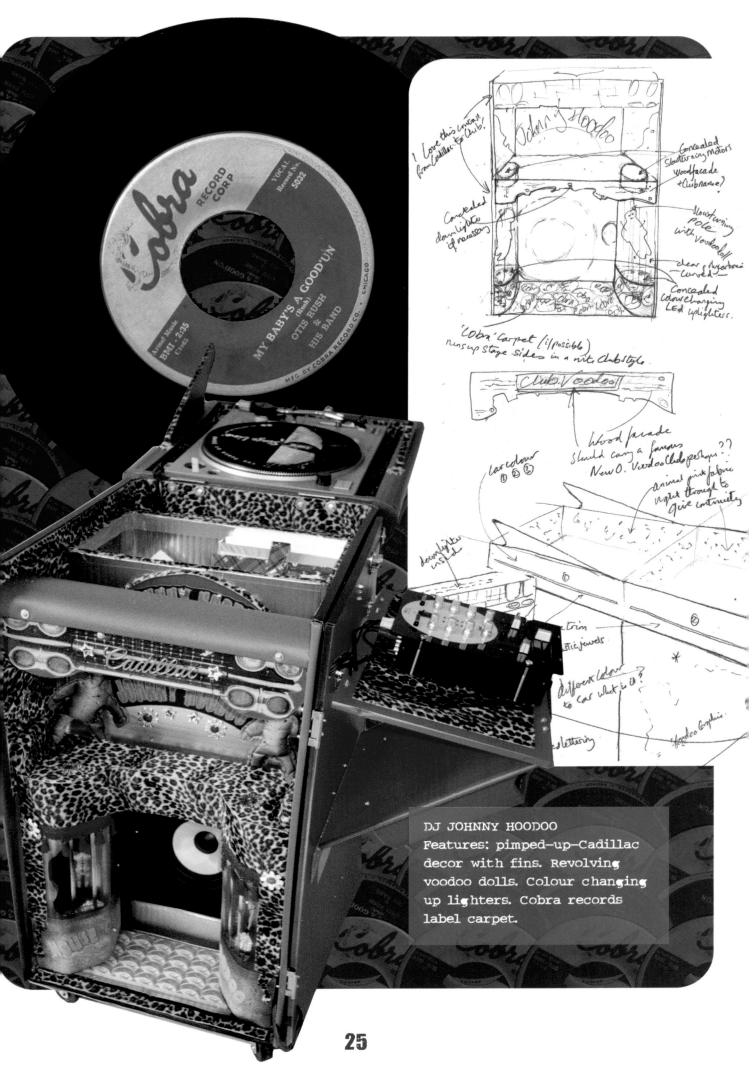

DJ JOHNNY HOODOO
Features: pimped-up-Cadillac
decor with fins. Revolving
voodoo dolls. Colour changing
up lighters. Cobra records
label carpet.

DJ BOOTLEGGER
Features: Rear mounted Captain's cabin. Drunken sailor tableau with rocking storm control. Off road wheels.

TUNNOCK'S
est 1890
Pride in our Products

Deejay Aye~

Pride in our Provincialness

CARAMEL

DJ AYE TUNES
Features: animated set of bag
pipes. Rotating Tunnock girl
Tunnock's tea cakes graphics.

DJ SOUNDS THAT SWING
Features: Upright position for
in shop display. Record fair and
in store listening facility for
CDs and vinyl.1950s pulp fiction
graphics.

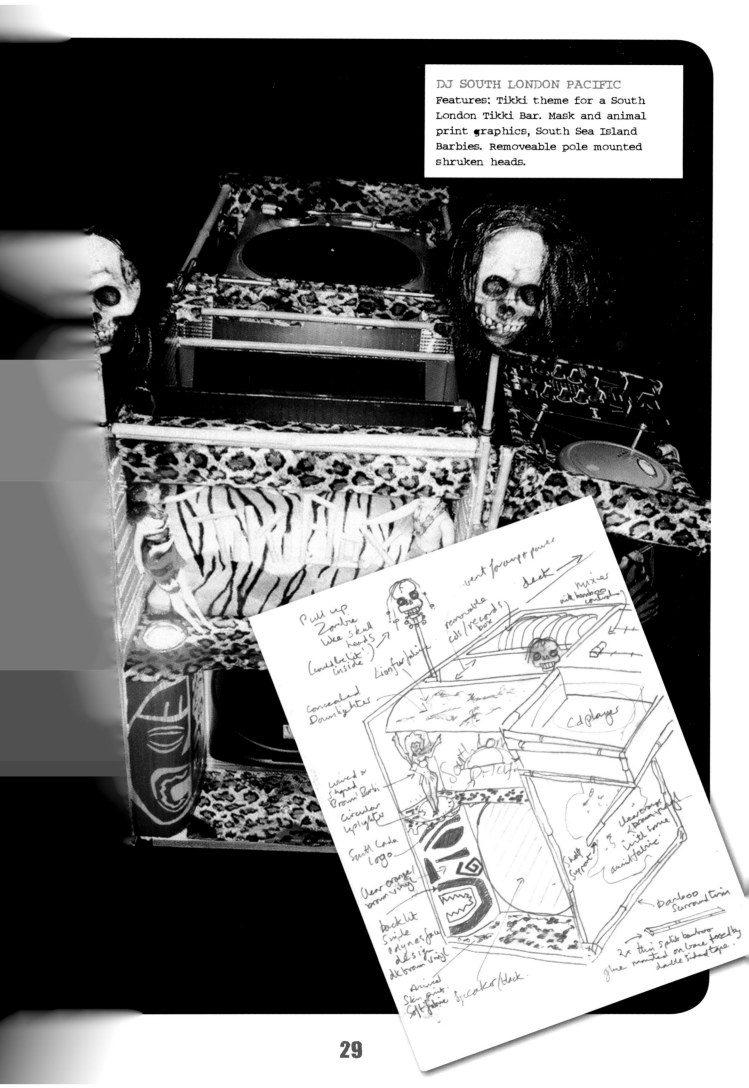

DJ SOUTH LONDON PACIFIC
Features: Tikki theme for a South London Tikki Bar. Mask and animal print graphics, South Sea Island Barbies. Removeable pole mounted shruken heads.

DJ LA TROLLEY BERGERE
Features: Side lit tattoo
logos. Burlesque theme.
Peep hole graphics.

DJ SONIC FRICTION
Features: Themed as a family of robots based in a future world. Graphics include robot wall paper and futurist predictions. Animated human servant moves forwards and back across the front of the machine.

DJ BIM BAM RECORDS
Features: Upright position for display. Record fair and in store listening facility for CDs and vinyl. Company logo and vinyl record label graphics.

DJ TREASURE ISLAND
Features: Jamie's own
personal Treasure Island.
Sand sea and palm trees.
'Underwater' revolving
Barbie mermaids.

DJ PUSSY CAT
Features: Late '50s cinema palace
theme. Removeable 'what's
showing tonight' cinema display
sign. Rear mounted light up
display panel for deck.

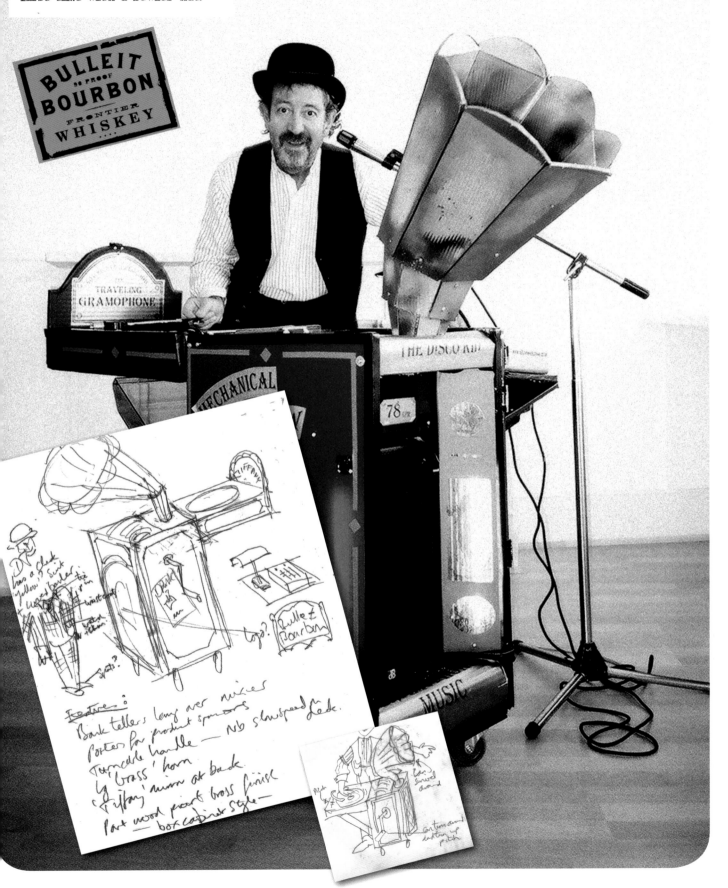

DJ THE DISCO KID
Features: Built for a Bourbon whiskey promotion. Vintage horn and wind up handle. My first time with a bowler hat.

Pickin' 'n' mixin'

HOW TO COMMISSION A WHEELIE BAG

Thanks to the versatility of 10mm polycarbonate Wheelie Bag construction has improved considerably since the old MDF days. Not so the measuring skills of its creator who persists in mistaking the number 16 for a 19 and for whom achieving a straight line is always a challenge. Since there was very little chance that one Wheelie Bag would ever turn out quite like another their uniqueness was established at the outset. The individual appearance and, indeed, personality of the various machines soon became one of the most interesting parts of the process. As far as possible each Wheelie Bag has its own theme and special features that reflect, at least in part, an original brief given by its future owner.

Commission for DJ Johnny Hoodoo
— as ordered by his girl friend.

' John is very particular about the cars he likes. I mean veeerrryyy particular, ie only certain years, models, versions, etc. I think it's best to keep it as general as possible... What about building him a 1965 — 1972 Wheelie-Cadillac for a New Orleans pimp who practices hoodoo and frequently visits Chicago to record tracks for Cobra records...'

Concealed slowturning motors
woodfacade + clubname?

slowturning pole with Voodoo!

'Cobra' Carpet
ns up stage sides in

Club

Close up and personal with:

DJ ROCK-OLA EDDY

I think you can trace the conception of my Wheelie Bag back to an idea I had a few years ago. It would try and recreate the jukebox from Malcolm McLaren's & Vivienne Westwood's 1970'S iconic Kings Road shop "SEX" (Too Fast To Live, Too Young To Die). I located the correct AMI jukebox at David Webb's wonderful Jukebox London showroom down at the Angel. However when I went down to inspect it I fell in love with a 1959 Rock-Ola Tempo instead, which looked like the back end of an electric blue Caddy sticking out of the wall. After purchasing it I joyfully went about stocking it and after the "SEX" collection was complete I embarked on tracking down all the "Born Bad" & "Songs The Cramps Taught Us" 45s. Vinyl fever had well and truly set in again! Then when "Sounds That Swing" moved their shop from Inverness Street onto Parkway directly opposite my shop, the occasional visit soon became a daily one with Barney, Neil and Olly only too happy to feed my addiction. Needless to say the collection swelled way past the capacity of the jukebox and an alternative means of playing them was needed. After listening to records on Barney's Wheelie Bag at the shop and enquiring where he got it, he introduced me to its creator at 'The Spread Eagle' and a new design idea was hatched.

The design process was a pleasure as he understood exacty what I wanted and was as enthusiastic as I was about it. In this case the spec was simply to make a portable Rock-Ola influenced machine with an extra matching deck for continuous music with an accompanying 'Burlesque Peep Show' featuring Betty Page.

All it needs now is some Cramps Wheelettes – so if anyone comes across a pair of Lux and Ivy dolls on their travels then please let me know!

Christian
Rock-Ola Eddy

Close up and personal with:

DJ THE COUNT

I have been a professional DJ and around the industry for many years and have a great love of all things vinyl and sound. I came across this brilliant machine flying home from a Christmas holiday in Penang. It was in one of the Malaysian Airlines in-flight magazines. It usually takes me ten minutes to read these mags but in this case I ripped the whole page out that contained the article on the great invention.

My design brief was a 1970s dusty Jamaican reggae sound system feel – just like the Trojan Record vans. We emailed a few pics and ideas back and forth a then "The Count" was born. The story behind The Count, is that this is my reggae DJ alias – this came about as a joke and has stuck for some time so I thought – I have to go with it on the machine. This was the easy part, next was getting it into Australia past customs.

I think from memory only two machines have been delivered in Oz and both were imported in as gifts, mine was the first one that was coming in as an overseas purchase. Finally I get the call that it has arrived in Melbourne and is sitting with Customs.

Then I get the phone calls… *What type of machine is this? Is this a CD player? Is this a sound system? Can you buy them off the shelf? What is it made out of? What type of light globes does it take? What wattage are they? What can you do with it?* In summary they could not find anything in their import classification book for it to fall under, the bottom line was that it meant a much lower duty for me as a result!

Anyway it was all part of my plan to have a mobile DJ rig for my move back to Tasmania. I have show cased the beauty on many occasions and it has been the focal point of the whole party many a time, people are gob smacked… even my dear grandmother who pesters me to play her jazz records out over the garden – classic! At the moment it is my outdoor festival machine at the flick of a switch, when the weather is good, I plug the unit in and sit it under an awning of the house and transmit across the garden, it's great. Thank goodness I went to Penang – that's all I can say!!

Brooke Allen
(Hobart Tasmania)

38

Close up and personal with:

DJ THE BOOTLEGGER

I have always longed to live near St Ives but I knew that I would regret not having access to regular Wheelie Bag events. I know some people end up buying a sports car as part of their mid-life crisis, why shouldn't I get four wheels of DJ vinyl playing power? During December 2009 and over my first Cornish Christmas I decide to go for it. Luckily I had kept my reasonably large and varied collection of 45s, although I did sell over 1500 LPs to help pay for my move, so at least I would not be short of some good singles to play. Also St Ives offered a fantastic regular event that I thought I might be able to contribute to, namely Bob Devereux's 'Frug'.

January brought an almost daily exchange of emails and before long we had decided on a pirate ship theme for my machine, based on my new location and in homage to my favourite British beat band of all time – The Pirates (of Mick Green and Johnny Kidd fame). This seemed to give plenty of design ideas with various sketches and plans. It was not long before we got into production even without a final name, that was to present itself at the very last moment. Numerous names were thought of but none seemed quite right until "The Bootlegger" – that was it! With both music and pirate/smuggling connotations it seemed ideal, plus it started me thinking of related song titles that I could use as my theme tunes.

I have now captained nearly 40 voyages/gigs with the Bootlegger mainly in the St Ives Bay area, although she has also been sighted on the south coast of Cornwall just off Mousehole. As well as the usual fortnightly sailings at the Frug, 'The Bootlegger' has also made voyages to local art gallery private views and parties, guested at various comedy and music events, and played its part at a notable birthday celebration for local St Ives artist Anthony Frost. She is also scheduled to act as a sound effects unit for the Denys Val Baker play "Cornwall for the Cornish" as part of this year's St Ives September Festival. As captain, I can report that she is still sailing and sounding as fine as ever. Here's hoping that you might witness the Bootlegger under full sail one day yourself.

The pitfalls of DJ-ing

Words: Moira Dennison Trolley: La Trolley Bergere Illustrations: Emily Hart

Let there be light.
When doing a spot of al fresco record playing there are some key points to note. During the day is fine; once the light fades grab that torch. Why stop there? Get yourself a standard lamp complete with tassled shade and bring a little style to the mix.

Gravity.
A trolley is built for travel, but dear reader remember these things. When venturing on the tube try not to get wedged between the doors. It is so unseemly. Getting to the venue by foot? What goes up hill does have a tendency to go downhill… very quickly. Something to do with gravity. Hold onto your trolley.

Boot space.
When buying a sports car with the boot space of a shoebox… do consider that a trolley has to fit in.

Never alone.
Living in a haunted Tudor cottage means you are never truely alone when spinning the vinyl.

Musical choice. La Trolley Bergere recommends: 'Leaving Rome' Jo Jo Bennett followed by Sex with Miss X.

Rollin' your own

HOW TO BUILD YOUR VERY OWN WHEELIE BAG

First off a word from Rex Standish otherwise known as DJ Tea Bag

'The Teabag is my own contribution to the world of Wheeliebaggery. Simply a less-than-sturdy and splinter-prone tea chest that I discovered in my grandmother's attic, powered by an unbranded 60-watt amp found on the street in Pimlico. I hesitate to reveal the most intimate details of its construction, lest I receive a visit from the Health and Safety Executive. Suffice it to say that, against all odds and the laws of physics, it has a magical empathy with vintage 45s that results in a throaty boom and crackle sufficient to enliven any social gathering. It is available for hire (cash only) for any licenced or unlicenced event prepared to risk it.'

Capt. R. Standish (RSJ, TCP, RPM)

Thanks Rex, but instead of a tea chest maybe you'd like to have a go at a fully fledged 'Sound Cruiser' using Polycarbonate for the construction. You'll find that '10mm twinwall' comes in all shapes and sizes. 10mm is obviously the thickness, twinwall means that it is made up of two surfaces with inner walls at 10mm intervals running the entire length of the sheet, like a honeycomb but only going one way. Polycarbonate can be cut or bent along the 'grain', which is easy or against the 'grain' which is a bit harder.

NOW FOR SOME HANDY TOOLS

Let's hear it for your local Pound Shop. Ever been in one? There are two leading brands Poundland (www.poundland.co.uk) and the 99p Store (www.99pstoreltd.com). Let's see what you get for £10: cutting knife, Phillips screwdriver, flat head screwdriver, long nosed pliers, scissors, metre rule, clamps, double sided tape, and masking tape. You'll also need the occasional use of an electric drill, a jig saw, a heat gun (usually used for paint stripping but is ideal for bending polycarbonate), a good supply of nuts, bolts and washers and a glue gun. You've probably already got a drill knocking about somewhere, you can actually cut the plastic with your cutting knife but it's safer to use a jigsaw (don't forget some ear mufflers), and the heat gun – well you definitely need one but the cheap and cheerful end of the range is fine for us.

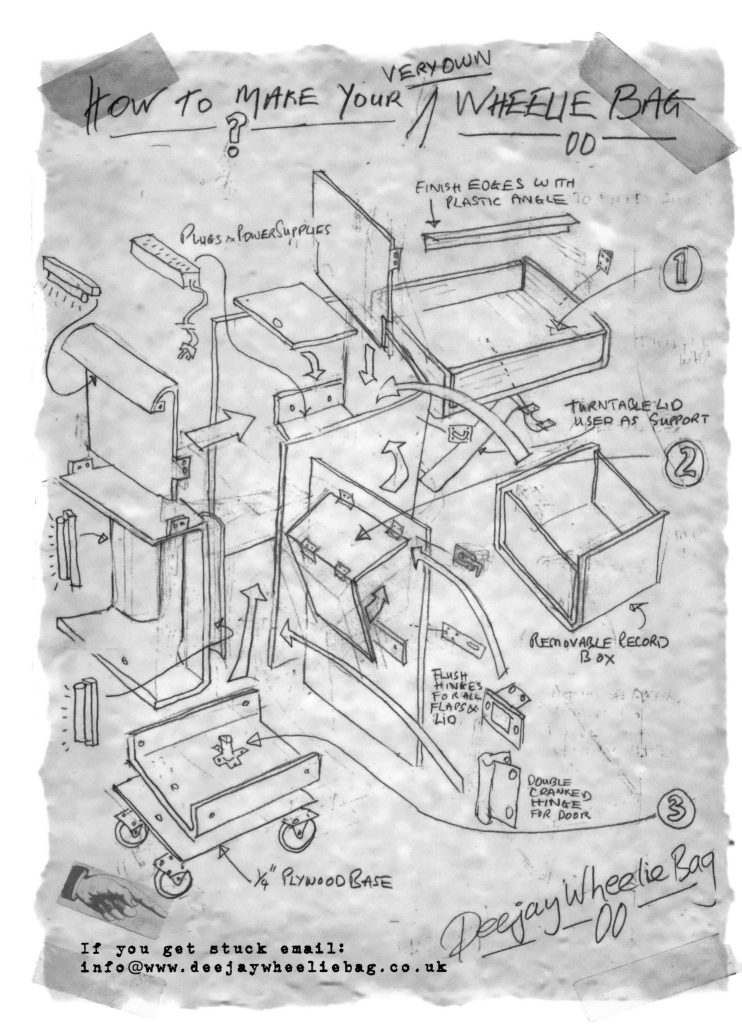

SOUNDSYSTEM

A tip from Deejay Wheelie Bag

It is best to purchase your equipment first before you work out the dimensions for your Wheelie Bag.

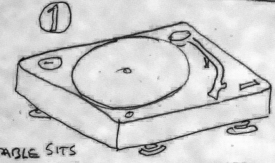

TURNTABLE SITS IN LID WHEN PLAYED

MIXER IS BOLTED TO DOOR FLAP

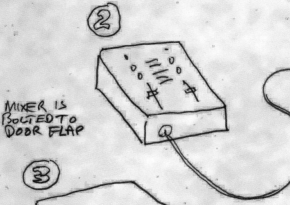

ACTIVE SPEAKER IS FIXED TO MIDDLE OF WHEEL BASE

Building a Wheelie Bag

CONSTRUCTION:
Use 10mm Twin Polycarbonate from www.polycarbonatedirect.co.uk When you order the Polycarbonate choose a wide sheet (2-3 metres) with a short length (1-1.5 metres) this will help you bend with the length of the twin wall rather than against it.

Fix together with nuts, bolts, washers and hinges available from www.screwfix.co.uk Use walls to thread audio leads.

Cover with coloured adhesive vinyl available from www.X-Film. co.uk or wwwthevinylcorporation. co.uk Mount on castor wheels available from www.castorcity.com

TOOLS NEEDED: Phillips screwdriver. Soldering iron. To cut the Polycarbonate use a jigsaw with a fine blade. To bend the Polycarbonate use a heat gun.

LIGHTING TRY: Link Lights available from www.linklights.co.uk Bolt light brackets to inner walls. Use coloured gel to create simple lighting effects.

HINGES: Use double crank hinges for the door. Use flush hinges elsewhere.

THE DECK: Try Stage Line DJP 102 from www.henrysaudio.co.uk. Use a light weight turntable that will comfortably fit in the Wheelie Bag when being transported. When playing place turntable in Wheelie Bag lid use turntable lid as a support.
Cut two holes at the back of the Wheelie Bag to take the lid hinges so that the lid rests against the Bag handle.

THE ACTIVE SPEAKER: Try American Audio from www.thedjshop.co.uk. Fit to wheel base bolt through the plywood for strength. Use dimpled rubber mat under speaker/deck to cut down vibration.

THE MIXER: Stage Line MPX from www.henrysaudio.co.uk Bolt mixer to fold up door panel. Check when folded down that it will fit in Wheelie Bag when door is closed.

The Wheelie Bag Ball

The Wheelie Bag Ball first began as a rather crowded affair on December 15th 2002 at "The Pillars of Hercules" in London's Soho. It was envisaged as a kind of showcase for both Wheelie Bag and owner. A demonstration of the indisputable link, in my mind, between owning a Wheelie Bag and the neccesity to perform with it. I initially threatened to buy back any Wheelie Bags from owners who failed to turn up. By year two the numbers attending the Ball had grown to the extent that it moved to The Midmay Working Men's Club where it was to remain for the next five or six years.

The opening of the Ball features a Grand Parade where the owners are judged upon how well they wheel their Wheelie Bag sound systems around the venue. A few cheery waves to members of the public could well score extra points. At this time the judges also make their decision regarding an award for the Best Dressed DJ.

The climax to the show is the Wheelie Bag Sound Clash. For this Wheelie Bag Deejays can select only two tracks upon which they are judged. Their use of the microphone and general ability to manage the Wheelie Bag controls is also assessed by the panel of judges. A variety of dramatic displays, fancy dress costumes and even the occasional burlesque performance have evolved as efforts to be top DJ have become ever more desperate, er I mean, inventive.

The Trolley Troubadour Trophy is awarded to the best DJ.

The closing ceremony of the first Wheelie Bag Ball. The DJs (for some reason missing The Caballo) gather for a final shot. As can be seen, I cope reasonably well with the embarrassment of winning my own prize.

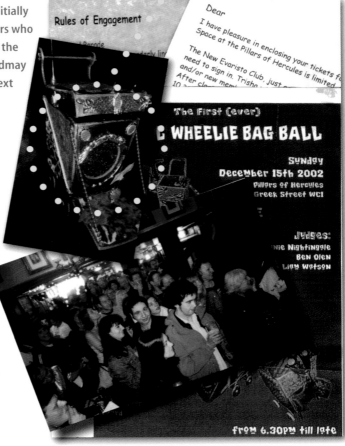

The crowd at the first Ball press forward, barely able to see the DJs let alone the Wheelie Bags, that's Annie Nightingale in the left hand corner.

Surely a winning combination.

Cheers, Deb.

Jasmine shares a magic moment.

End of the line for the Phatt Controller as Night Train self destructs!

Silence proves golden for Ben.

Tom, Singles Bar, with loyal posse in support.

Why no mirrors Dave? Dunno Smiler, maybe we'll have to bump start it.

Come back Annie we miss you.

G'day mate this is Perth calling the Flying Doctor.

Long night ahead eh, Richard.

The Magpie DJ and some, er… friends.

Anyone know how this works?

C'mon Ben we know you're in there.

A touchy feely moment of triumph for team Caballo.

Nice tie Liam but why the missing door?

The Phatt Controller finally gets to lead the Parade.

The Performing Hat makes its one and only appearance.

Sorry Tea bag your time will come.

46

Completely off their trolleys

It's a wet Sunday night, and I'm in the Mildmay Club on Newington Green in Dalston, and, although I might be suffering from a cold, surely it hasn't reached the hallucinatory fever stage? In front of me, grown men and women are pushing shopping trolleys around, each one adapted to carry a speaker and turntable, and customised to illustrate a theme relevant to their owner. I realise that I'm sitting behind a desk on a stage, and despite my worst misgivings, seem to be fully clothed ...

That's a relief then, for it means I'm at the second annual Wheelie-Bag Ball, invited as a judge rather than trapped in a dream (though I appreciate that many of you will think I'm making this up).

The original DJ Wheelie Bag is Denys, a sometime photography lecturer from north London. He has a sideline as a maker of ultra-portable DJ equipment, strictly mono, which fits neatly into an easily transported apparatus based on the oversized devices dragged by old ladies through crowded shopping streets, hence the name.

Every year he invites the owners of his machines to the ball, mercifully this year held in a more practical venue than the cramped Soho pub, The Pillars of Hercules, site of his Wednesday night residency. So far, 16 of the contraptions have been delivered, and shouts were sent out across the globe, to places as distant as Amsterdam, Perth in Western Australia, and Norwich, for this celebration of wheeliness. Eleven are

here, although sadly "Night Train" has arrived in less than pristine condition after its owner, Maggi, totalled it within yards of the venue.

The evening began with the Grand Parade and a prize for "best vehicular control sponsored by Mr and Mrs Madhar of MLB Handbags (and trolleys) of Ridley Rd Market". By dint of her red beret and ability to manage heel kicks with controlled forward motion, Debbie won a nylon laundry bag. Best-dressed entrants were Noah and Johnny, a duo operating "Flat Dogs", one dressed in hippie lumberjack garb, the other in a linen suit and what can only be described as a tropical *pickelhaube*, but shirtless nonetheless. The one-off T-shirt had to be his.

This was no more than a preamble to the main event, a sound clash for the "Trolley Troubadour Award". Each entrant played two tunes, marks awarded (sort of) for choice of music, use of microphone (tricky this) and the changeover technique (wheelies have only one deck). Such strict criteria meant that the judges had to ignore such tricks as Debbie's turntable of fire, using lighter fuel and an old copy of Shocking Blue's "Venus", or the re-enaction of that Run DMC/Aerosmith video by Henry and Tim.

In the end, Noah and Johnny won. Their slot had everything – one song you knew, one you didn't but wouldn't mind hearing again, some spontaneous microphone work, children dancing and a right good hoedown atmosphere. But frankly, everyone was great, even though Denys's latest creation, a battery-powered picnic basket-cum-record player, failed to work.

Steve Jelbert

DJ COOL

AND HOW NOT TO LOSE IT AT THE WHEELIE BAG BALL

To my easily excited mind the Annual Sound Clash is a celebration of music, individuality, and the Wheelie Bag in all of its unique flavours. Believe me, standing in front of a hundred plus people and spinning a couple of discs is a nerve racking experience. Far better to make the time go quickly and get it over with by putting together a performance linked to your choice of records. With a bit of planning you may not only amuse the crowd but also be in with a chance of lifting the trophy.

Though you may have the rarest and most brain destroying records in Wheelie Bagdom there is nothing more challenging for an audience than to watch you spin them while sitting down and scratching your chin. You will not be thanked. So put your Johnny B. Cool persona in a box for a few minutes and get ready to make a fool of yourself. Your friends will still talk to you afterwards. In fact you may also make some new ones too. First, choose a couple of records that complement one another. Then try and think about the potential that each offers for the use of props and generally acting the fool.

'Tied up? Yes please — ready when you are Mr Garageman.'

'WHY NOT SELECT SOMEONE AT RANDOM... AND TIE THEM UP?'

I'M A DJ, GET ME OUT OF HERE

The easiest approach I find is to choose a theme. This should be easy if you have boxes and boxes of 45s cluttering the house and annoying a partner.

Let us take for example the theme of "Cowboys and Indians". There are literally hundreds, possibly thousands, of songs about The Wild West. In this instance we are going to use "Davey Crockett" by Thee Headcoatees followed by an instrumental entitled "Too Much Firewater" by Lorenzo Smith on the Mar-Vel label. The first is the perfect synthesis of The Ramones "Gabba Gabba Hey" chant and "Farmer John" by The Premiers while the latter features lots whooping and hollering. Talk about musical nirvana. Now find yourself a Davey Crockett hat (not easy) and on a wet afternoon make a "Gabba Gabba Hey" sign and attach it to a broom handle. You are correct, while the first record plays you are going to parade around the room like Joey Ramone and encourage people to sing along. Then, moments after you have changed discs (see below for unhelpful advice), you are going to discard the furry hat and dig out a Red Indian headdress.

You will be amazed at what can be hidden in a Wheelie Bag but I digress. Accompanying props might include a hatchet, thereby providing an opportunity for you to fulfil your Screamin' Lord Sutch fantasy, or a length of rope. Why not select someone at random, though not a member of the judging panel, and tie them up? However, my advice is to prearrange something with a consenting adult if you do not want to get arrested.

So that's the choice of music and the performance bit sorted out. Easy! But how do you use a microphone effectively and what about the changeover technique between platters? Not easy. My advice is to put egg trays on your living rooms walls and to practice, practice, and practice. For the time being throw caution to the wind and bluff it. You never know the crowd might still be in shock from the first three minutes and fail to notice your shaky hands and the howl of feedback filling the room. But to hell with it, continue to act like a madman for another three minutes and before you can shout "I'm a DJ, get me out of here." the ordeal will be over.

Good luck and may your castors never fall off en route to the venue.

LIVIN' THE LIFE

Are you an ATTIC FANATIC?

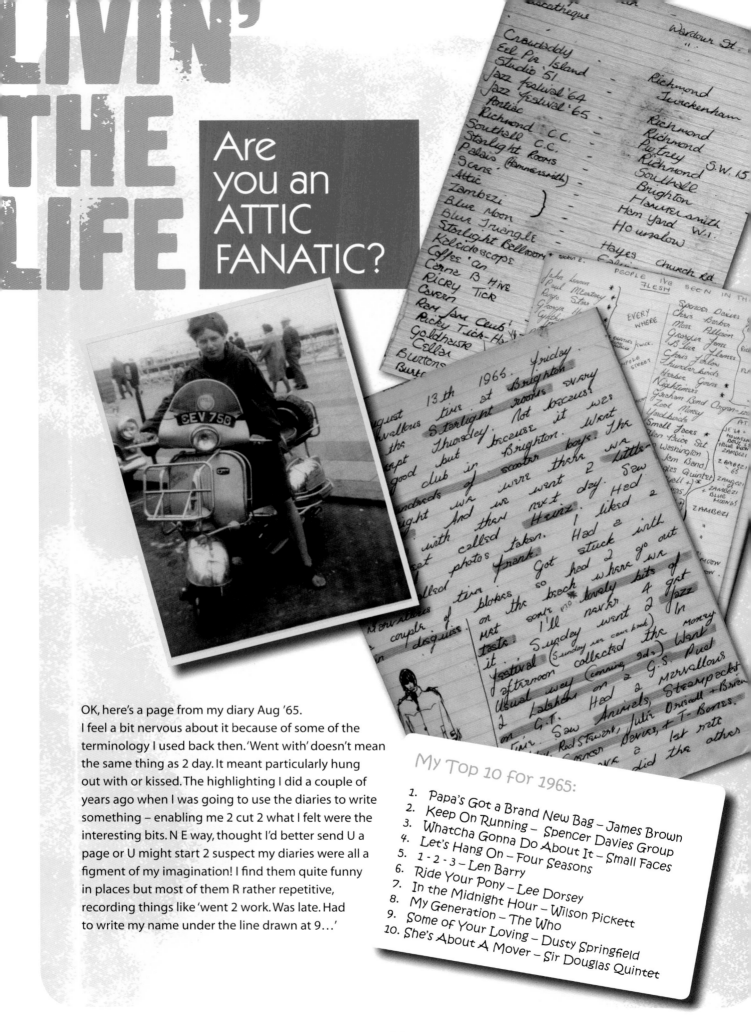

OK, here's a page from my diary Aug '65.
I feel a bit nervous about it because of some of the
terminology I used back then. 'Went with' doesn't mean
the same thing as 2 day. It meant particularly hung
out with or kissed. The highlighting I did a couple of
years ago when I was going to use the diaries to write
something – enabling me 2 cut 2 what I felt were the
interesting bits. N E way, thought I'd better send U a
page or U might start 2 suspect my diaries were all a
figment of my imagination! I find them quite funny
in places but most of them R rather repetitive,
recording things like 'went 2 work. Was late. Had
to write my name under the line drawn at 9…'

My Top 10 for 1965:

1. Papa's Got a Brand New Bag – James Brown
2. Keep On Running – Spencer Davies Group
3. Whatcha Gonna Do About It – Small Faces
4. Let's Hang On – Four Seasons
5. 1 - 2 - 3 – Len Barry
6. Ride Your Pony – Lee Dorsey
7. In the Midnight Hour – Wilson Pickett
8. My Generation – The Who
9. Some of Your Loving – Dusty Springfield
10. She's About A Mover – Sir Douglas Quintet

'Waddya think?' he said with an air of confidence that fell someway short of being shared by his Director. 'Who's going to be in it?' said Geraldine as they looked round the venue, 'You need some celebrities'.

'Na, don't worry about that', said Wheelie. 'Got loads of 'em.' He pulled out a crumpled piece of paper from his pocket. 'Oihane and the Punks, Lewis an' the Hot Licks, Dave an' the Mod Squad, Mama Con Yuka with the Latin Crew, an' lots of judges, Gene Serene, Florence from Kiss of Fire, Nick from Intoxica an' Bruce 'Bash' Brand the drummer. Bruce 'as been in loadsa bands', he added aware that his list had made little impact on the Director.

Deejay Wheelie Bag Presents:
SOUND ME OUT!
The FINAL Showdown!

RHYTHM AND BLUES
Kitty Daisy & Lewis
LATIN BEATS
MAMA CON YUKA
PUNK ROCK
Oihane & The Punks
BRITISH BEAT
DAVE AND THE MOD SQUAD
Sound Me Out! Panel
Florence, Gene, Bruce & Nick
with Lovely Les as the Show Assistant
Sunday 19th September 3.00pm
The People Show Theatre Pollard Row London E2

'What is that?' she replied pointing an accusing finger at a gold painted plastic ear attached to a wooden base. 'That's the prize, made it myself, gonna call it the Golden Lobe Award'. 'Ok and the script, where's the script?' 'Er… , the script. Well some tv programmes 'ave 'em an' some don't. This is one of 'em that don't 'ave one', he replied. 'Well I need to plan some shots. Can you please do whatever it is you're going to do to that table over there?' 'There's nobody at the table'. 'Well I'm sure that won't bother a host who doesn't need a script', she replied from behind a camera. Wheelie spent the next two hours talking to a number of empty tables, two or three empty chairs and a rather elegant hat-stand that stood in for one of the judges. 'Cool', said Debbie, 'Love the table cloths!'

The next day Wheelie arrived at the venue to find it transformed with a vast array of equipment, leads, lights and cameras.

'Don't worry I blagged most of it', smiled Producer Debbie as she tried to reassure her host who was suddenly looking rather nervous.

For the first time Wheelie wondered what would happen if things did not go according to plan. He took up his place beside the Wheelie Bag he had built specially for the occasion.

'What do you think of my audience?' said Johnny Hoodoo.

Wheelie gazed at a colourful and excited crowd now seating themselves. The DJs and their friends had all turned up, the judges too. 'Quiet please,' came the commanding voice of Geraldiine taking control. 'Sound turning' said a guy with headphones on. The room went quiet, a camera on a long jib wormed it's way down towards Wheelie. 'Take one' called a man with a clapper board.

'TAKE ONE!'

Wheelie's mind went blank 'Er…' was all he managed not sure if he should stand up or sit down. 'Cut', called Geraldine

'TAKE TWO!'

'Er thanks for comin' an' that', said Wheelie rising to his feet, he decided to hold his arms up, 'Er… let's hear it for Sound Me Out!' Much to his surprise there was a loud applause.

It was going to be alright.

Les spun the arms of The Clash Determinator, the DJs chose their music, the judges gave their opinions and the audience dutifully cheered every time a 'clash' went to the vote. In the end Dave and The Mod Squad won and gratefully received their Golden Lobe Award. 'Well you finally got to do it', said Lewis, he had flown in from France with his Hot Licks to attend. 'Yes', said Wheelie, 'I think we did'.

Wheelie put 'Television Companies' into Google a vast amount of information came up, he wrote down some numbers. 'Who did you say you were?' said a surprised Creative Director, taken off guard for a moment by his direct line ringing. 'I'm Deejay Wheelie Bag an' I'm callin' you up 'cos I've got a really good programme for your television channel. It's much better than other programmes an' I'm sure you'll like it'.

'How did you get this number?', the Director replied. 'I'm gonna be in your area next week an' I'll be able to make a personal appearance at your Television Studio next Friday'. 'Please do not do that', said the Director, we have no interest in unsolicited material', he paused, 'and there is nobody here on Fridays' he added with an air of finality. 'I've also built you a scale replica of my 'Clash Determinator' what we used in the programme', continued Wheelie unabated. 'An' if Friday's no good I'll come on Thursday'.

Wheelie put the phone down and copied the Managing Director of the company into an email regarding the visit plus a picture of the scale model. Unaware of the previous conversation the MD's secretary confirmed the meeting and booked a room.

The sight of the 60 year old DJ, attired in a Teddy Boy drape, eating a pork pie he's bought on the way from the station provided more than sufficient reason for Wheelie Bag to be hurried through from the studio's reception area into the Creative Director's office.

'Five minutes' said the young executive barely looking up from his desk 'how the Hell you got in here, I don't know'. 'Well I bet you liked it' said his optimistic visitor. 'Only had time to watch the trailer I'm afraid. Bit niche for us', he added. 'What does that mean', enquired Wheelie frustrated at DJ Ben's prediction coming true.

'Well it's not for us, but it's not a bad idea'. He paused. 'Leave it with us we'll pitch it to MTV'.

On the strength of his result at the television studio Wheelie went ahead and booked a premier of the show in his favourite pub. Everyone said they would come along and on the night the pub was taken over by an exotic assortment of DJs, Mods, Rockabillies, would be film producers and assorted friends.

Unfortunately for Wheelie that same morning he had heard back from the television man. 'Sadly, at our meeting with MTV today we were informed that the station is no longer interested in commissioning new music shows, they prefer a more 'life style' approach such as 'Underage and pregnant' and 'Teenage Dads'.

It was Wheelie's turn to be surprised and exasperated.

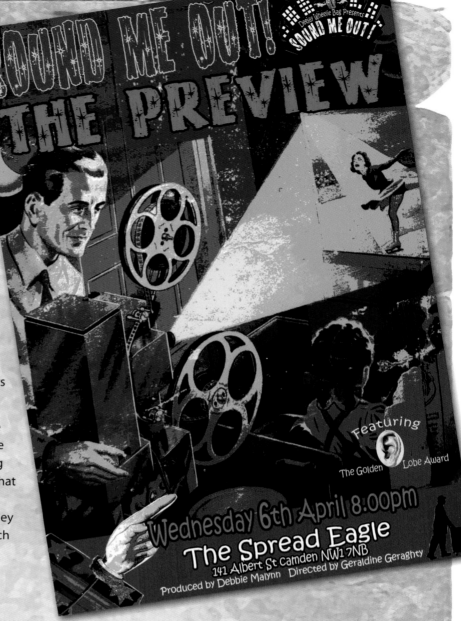

SOMETIME LATER...

Wheelie smiled as he remembered the night before. The film had gone down well, he'd thanked everyone for watching and helping to make the idea become a reality. There were many things that he wanted to say (no change there then). What he did eventually say came as a bit of a surprise.

'We'll not be sellin' it to MTV after all', he announced. He looked around at a pub full of great friends, he looked at his beer for inspiration.

He rose to the occasion. 'Films like ours about music, about people who play music an' er, people who just enjoy music, well it's like this, it's a bit too niche for 'em'.

Findin' 'n' buyin'

BUYING RECORDS IN ATHENS – MORE THAN A MYTH

It's 3.00pm on Friday afternoon, my flight out of Athens is at 6.00pm. I have decided that I just have time for a quick visit to a record shop near Monasteraki market run by a guy called Makis. The shop is no bigger than a corridor, I am sorting through 50 records or so that I have taken from a shelf with about 500 more still to go, they are in no order with no covers.

Apparently there was a riot in the street the night before, someone has now kicked over a tear gas canister, the street is full of an acrid smelling smoke. People are squeezing into the shop to avoid the smell. I have my hat over my nose and mouth. Everyone is coughing. I have found a record called 'Le beau tetard sur son cigar' by Les Marylennes (it turned out to be a great track owing not a little to 'Ce plain pour moi' by Plastic Bertrand).

From across the crowded shop comes the voice of the owner. 'Hey! Englishman what you think of this Tony Blair?' I mumble something through my hat like 'I don't know and I don't much care'. 'He's the fucking bastard that caused all this trouble', my host continued and the rest of the shop quickly agreed.

I offered up my few purchases and tried to laugh. Nobody else seemed to share the joke.

On my way through Athens centre there's a shop I always pass that is brim full of vinyl but from which I have unfortunately been banned. The owner objected to my use of a portable record player to cherry pick his vast but unsorted stock of 45s. 'Next time you in my shop no record player' he tells me. To which I reply that without the player I cannot check the records. 'Ok', he says, 'No record player and no you'.

Today, as ever, he stands just inside the doorway. I'm still banned and the shop remains as mysterious and as short of customers as when I first found it.

I walk on up the hill to Vinyl City. In the attic of this rough and ready corner shop are in excess of 10,000 vinyl 45s.

They are in tall wobbly piles, no covers and definitely no particular order. You have to check everyone. It takes me about four to five hours to complete about 1,500 records. I have been going for about two years now.

On this occasion I retrieve 'Big long slidin' thing' by Dinah Washington and an early Ella Fitzgerald along with an assorted bunch of the kind of odd stuff I love including a couple of Chicago Polkas and a record about Elvis describing what it's like to be in Heaven.

There are a lot of theories about why certain types of records crop up where they do. American airbases in the East of England, transatlantic shipping and the Port of Liverpool, Jamaican immigrants and the London club scene, sure these factors made for the variety of the world's music found in the UK. But the reason for so many boxes, well often just piles, of records cluttering the pavements of an Athen's Sunday market is beyond me. Of course a lot of them are Greek records but, defying any logical explanation, a vast number, most certainly, are not!

I climb down the attic ladder back into the shop. The owner asks me if I've had a good day. I say yes and happily part with a Euro apiece for my hard won trophies.

'Did you see the ones in the window?', he comments in a rough chain smoker's voice. 'Yes I did them last year', I politely reply looking across at the ominous four foot high black shiney stacks . 'What about the shelves?' he continues, I nod 'Yeah them too'. He is unmoved by my dedication 'And the washroom?'. Somewhat surprised I look down at my dirt blackened hands the result of a four hour shift, I was not even aware that there was a washroom. 'There's another 4,000 in there. Do them when you come back next time eh!' he winks. I make my way to the door. 'Are you interested in American 78s?' he adds.

Four weeks later on a hot afternoon in June I returned to check out the toilet stash. There were indeed two or three thousand records piled up behind the bowl but it was hot and cramped in there. Undetered I tried not to think of where I was and got on with the task ahead. I found 'The Monkey Time' by Major Lance and felt encouraged but replacing handfuls of records back on the floor meant my head practically entering the toilet each time I did so.

The elderly owner of the shop was the other side of the door, he appeared to be talking to a young relative but he spoke in English, I caught a phrase or two. 'Well my dear please show me more of the tattoo'. I was intrigued but having gone to so much trouble to get into the toilet I could not allow myself to stop and go out.

My persistence paid off. I found an amazing track called 'Tokyo Boogie Woogie' recorded in 1946 by the Tokyo Orchestra with its famous singer the actress Shizuko Kasagi. With about 50 records I eventually emerged. The owner was in fact on the shop's computer Skyping with a young girl from Thailand.

I paid up and walked out on what was left of a beautiful sunny afternoon. The quaint, tree lined, street tipped steeply down hill . At every junction stood a group of riot police.

How about that miniature torch you always wanted, or something for the lady? Check out these shopping trolley traders when you arrive at the Athens Bus Station.

Wheelin' 'n' dealin'

GAMES THAT PEOPLE PLAY

It is difficult to remain too serious when playing music out of a wheel-around box themed up to look like a giant insect or a Voodoo Cadillac. Games, or interventions help to build up a show and break away from the normal DJ format. Everyone thinks that they know all about games and that all games are like Bingo. A good game however will act like a piece of cabaret turning the evening on its head, creating a little anarchy along the way. New games are unexpected and come as a surprise to a generation fixated with 'coolness'. Try 'Escape from the Tyranny and Oppression of Capitalistic Imperialism.' Buy a box of 6 inch rubber bands, give out a dozen. Announce that the winner will be the first to 'escape' by climbing through the rubber band.

Then there are dice games, these depend on you calling out numbers, 'Ah just like Bingo' you say. Well yes, if you like, but the way is wide open to play around with this genre and invent some neat alternatives of our own. Here's one of mine that I have called 'Day of the Dead'. It has some intriguing characters such as Scarey Mary, Mr Dead Lucky and Tequila Tom and has been specially illustrated for the Annual by Vince Ray. The boards can be easily photocopied in black and white. When printed fold the three A4 sheets down the middle and carefully cut between each of the characters, divide the games in half and you are ready to go. Tell your audience to fold each character up when they hear its number called out (thus bringing them back from the dead). I use two dice at a time. Tell everyone that if a board has a number repeated (and they all have) they must hear this number called twice in order to raise both figures. The two dice and the use of doubles keeps the game going longer and is less predictable. Confused? You'll get the hang of it, and anyway your audience need to be puzzled to make sure that they pay attention!

JOHNNY VOODOO   MISS REAPER   Mr. DEAD LUCKY   ZOMBIE BRIDE   SCAREY MARY   TEQUILA TOM

2 1 4 2 5 1

DEEJAY WHEELIE BAG'S
DAY OF THE DEAD
www.deejaywheeliebag.co.uk

www.deejaywheeliebag.co.uk
DAY OF THE DEAD
DEEJAY WHEELIE BAG'S

4 1 & 2 & 1

TEQUILA TOM   SCAREY MARY   ZOMBIE BRIDE   Mr. DEAD LUCKY   MISS REAPER   JOHNNY VOODOO

JOHNNY VOODOO · MISS REAPER · Mr. DEAD LUCKY · ZOMBIE BRIDE · SCAREY MARY · TEQUILA TOM

DEEJAY WHEELIE BAG'S
DAY OF THE DEAD
www.deejaywheeliebag.co.uk

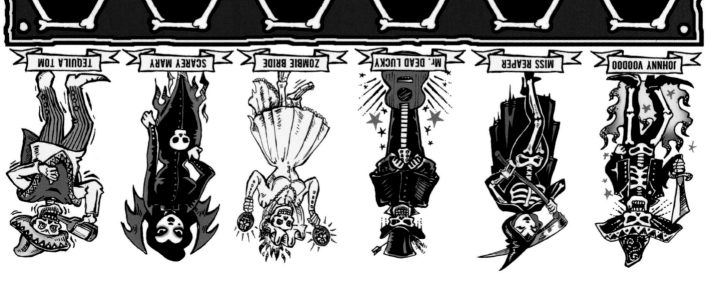

JOHNNY VOODOO   MISS REAPER   Mr. DEAD LUCKY   ZOMBIE BRIDE   SCAREY MARY   TEQUILA TOM

6 4 1 6 4 3

DEEJAY WHEELIE BAG'S
DAY OF THE DEAD
www.deejaywheeliebag.co.uk

www.deejaywheeliebag.co.uk
DAY OF THE DEAD
DEEJAY WHEELIE BAG'S

5 4 6 5 4 1

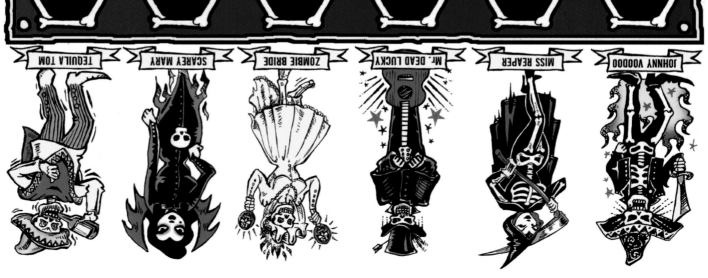

TEQUILA TOM   SCAREY MARY   ZOMBIE BRIDE   Mr. DEAD LUCKY   MISS REAPER   JOHNNY VOODOO

Dunroamin'

REVEALING THE WHEELIE BAG RELICS

Worn out, replaced, passed on, but where are they now?

DJ Jon takes delivery of Wheelitzer#1 Norwich Station 2001

... some years later

New owner Helen, Wheelie Bag and baby under the stairs Norwich 2011

THE FIRST WHEELIE BAG TO BE COMMISSIONED

The Wheelitzer#1 was delivered to Norwich late in 2001. Passed on when Wheelitzer#2 arrived, it presently resides next to a Dyson in an under-stairs cupboard. The early machine is still in working order and is now in the tender loving care of DJ Helen (Hell on Wheels) who will return to deejaying when her hands are less full.

Hot licks from Debbie Does.

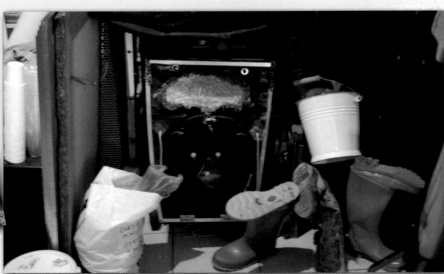

DJ Debbie Does, a Trolley Troubadour Award Winner, retains her original machine alongside her Wellington boots and by the looks of it some fold up chairs and a bucket. Having survived numerous party bookings and various attempts to set her deck on fire this playful machine eventually lost it in the wheel department and had to be replaced.

DJ Jon with Wheelitzer#2
in full, er, flow perhaps?
2004.

Jon's third machine, Wheelitzer#3 – a Sound Cruiser, is still
going strong, however it meant the passing on of #2. This trusty
combination of MDF, glitter balls and undersea frogmen was
passed on to DJ(?) Tim in whose care and back room it remains to
this day. To my knowledge Tim is still to receive his Wheelie Bag
training (come on Jon) but to be fair it looks like you remebered
where it was Tim, so that's a start I guess.

Wheelie in a thoughtful
mood, Mildmay Working
Men's Club 2004.

This splendid machine saw me through many a weekly session
at The Pillars of Hercules. Its separate amplifier had a habit of
falling out the back but the speaker sound was great. Now in the
company of scooters and Mods its graphics may be a tad too rock
'n' roll for their taste. Fred Perry make over please Smiler.

MEET THE RELATIVES: 1
Jasmine and the Magic Mini Bags

Looking back I don't know what it was that I first fell for… was it the beauty? the strength? the sheer razzmatazz? No matter, in any case I knew that my life was forever changed… without question, without thought of any kind I had to have IT… MY OWN WHEELIE BAG, MY OWN PIECE OF DJing Genius. That's all history now. The first Wheelie Bag – Old Blighty – has gone to the Wheelie Bag heaven in the sky. It was made of MDF, bits of metal, odd bits of other things, and was tied onto the back of a trolley. I wheeled it up and down stairs in the underground, onto buses and onto trains. I united Londoners and unsuspecting tourists alike by forcing them to help me. I took it to posh restaurants and council estates. I lost so much weight I've never looked so good in my life. I fleetingly thought of setting out my own fitness video entitled: 'If you truly want to lose weight and become really toned then own a Wheelie Bag made of MDF and wheel it around London 5 times a week'.

Jasmine at The Magic Circle Club 2004.

73

I continued with my gigs doing children's parties for two years but when I became happily pregnant I didn't know what to do with my Wheelie Bag relationship. Then a lightbulb flashed bright in my mind, if I can have a baby so too can my Wheelie Bag! Together we can multiply and go forth into the world with new life. So here we are 7 years later, my daughter Jasmine the catalyst for the future of 'Jasmine's Magic Parties'.

Along this exciting journey we have been joined by Dhillon, my son and four other Wheeliebagettes (all come with exciting new girl fairies/princesses/ or whatever you want them to be). Together we are the new generation of performers, bringing music, excitement, art and performance to children's parties around the London and Greater London area… Thank you and Goodbye.'

Jasmine, Nadia and Jasmine Jnr 2011.

How to use a Mini Magic Bag. Demonstration by Jasmine Jnr.

MEET THE RELATIVES: 2
Portmanteau Bag

RELATIVE: 3
Maria's Maquina Maraca
Queen of the carpark DJs

FOR ONE NIGHT ONLY

Play and display – Posters on parade

As well as a Wheelie Bag, a few records and a game or two any decent DJ needs a poster to promote the next performance. It's worth visiting the venue first and seeing for yourself where a poster could go to best attract attention. Get the agreement of the venue, they might even pay for the printing. Stick the design on a pen drive and drop it round to a digital printer. A good size full colour job is less than you'd think and makes all the difference, try www.onlinerepro.co.uk

CRAZY HOMIES Present Cinco de Mayo Music Festival Thursday 5th May RED HOT LATIN BEATS With Deejay Whee... Crazy Competitions Pound Shop Prizes Electric Dancing Girls From ... Crazy Homies

Sound... Swing & The Spread E... Present Deejay Wheelie Bag's WINTER WARMER Flamin Grooves Rockin Vinyl Scorchin Ska Sizzlin Latin Licks THE HOT ONE! Wednesday 5th Jan Crazy competitions Pound Shop Prizes Electric Dancing Girls FROM 7.30 The Spread Eagle 141 Albert St Camden NW1 7NB

THE BIG CHILL HOUSE Deejay Wheelie Bag SUNDAY SHOW Electric Dancing Girls Crazy Competitions Pound Shop Prizes FREE! Every Sunday 2.00 - 6.00pm GREAT FOOD all day Afternoon Kids' Menu & Juice Bar Authentic RnB - Rockabilly - Ska - Big Chill House : Kings X tube & rail Right next to Thameslink Stn. 257-259 Pentonville Rd, Kings Cross London N1 9NL Living etc

Deeja... & the... Barbican March 6th ...omething Different! ...ROCKING ...E SHOW... ...ions ...es ...irls ...pm 'Brilliant' Time Out 'Ahead of it's time' A Einstein 'Nice set of wheels' ebay.com www.deejaywheeliebag.co.uk

Sounds that Swing & The Spread Eagle Present Mid Summer Madness WEDNESDAY 6th JULY With Deejay Wheelie Bag Crazy Competitions Pound Shop Prizes Electric Dancing Girls From 7.30pm, till late. The Spread Eagle 141 Albert St Camden NW1 7NB

One for the Road

HOW I CASTOR MY SPELL WITH DJ JOHNNY HOODOO

Once the Wheelie Bag controls have been mastered with opening and shutting, lifting and wheeling techniques coming naturally it could be time to hit the road. Thanks to the sophisticated technology of four wheels and a handle the Wheelie Bag makes an ideal companion should an owner ever be lured away to exotic gigs in far flung places. Take this example from DJ Johnny Hoodoo (45) and DJ Elliot (78).

By email. The event was the 15th rockabilly rave 20th june at camber sands pontins middle of no where , england... jj

Thanks Mr Hoodoo, tough call between journalism or dance instructor, I can see that.

One for the Road

Shrine on with DJ Mama con Yuca

In the case of DJ Mama Con Yuca (this year's Wheelie Bag Sound Clash Winner) her 'Shrine' themed Wheelie Bag components made it all the way to Venezuela. Unfortunately the return journey was a different story when customs removed evey last nut and bolt. 'They even broke open the plaster figures, the National Guards looked at me like psychos, they enjoy it'. Shrine on Mama, shrine on.

RIP

DOCTOR VINYL AND THE CABINET OF CURIOUS DESIRE

The only Wheelie Bag to be rejected by its potential owners.

It went on to underwhelm the panel of judges at the Norwich Turnip Prize.

It was eventually dumped in 2010.

Acknowledgements

Scott Chasserot Wheelie Bag portraits p.12-20

Lynda Nyland Wheelie Bag Ball pics p.41, 47 and 51

Chris Avis Wheelie Bag portaits and relic shots

Design: GloryHall.com

Print: Ylolfa.com

And all you wonderful Wheelie Bag Owners who contributed.

Many thanks.

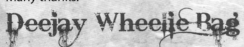

SUFFOLK AND WATT

Suffolk and Watt publisher
ISBN-978-0-9545985-4-9
Published in 2011 by Suffolk and Watt
© D. Avis, 2011
www.deejaywheeliebag.co.uk

PS. The Magpie Wheeler. Stay away from this man. Without a Wheelie Bag of his own he likes to perch in someone else's. He's even got his own wheels so be warned!

PPS. Get more copies of this Annual at: www.deejaywheeliebag.co.uk/annual

THE WHEELIE BAG DJ
HALL OF FAME

1. Wheelie Bag Mk 1
2. Wheelitzer Mk1
3. Nite Train Mk 1
4. Zombie Zoo
5. Wheelie Bag Mk2
6. Flat Dogs
7. Scarab
8. MC Royale
9. Caballo
10. Debbie Does Mk 1
11. Wheelitzer Mk 2
12. Marconi
13. Veneer
14. Jasmines Magic Parties
15. Wheelie Bag Mk 3
16. Cadillac
17. Woodland Creatures
18. Tiki Box
19. Smirnoff Vodka
20. Mod Squad
21. Singles Bar
22. Pussy Cat Palace
23. Portmanteau
24. Rock Circus
25. Wheelitzer Mk 3
26. Treasure Island
27. Bulleit Bourbon
28. Aye Tunes
29. Sounds That Swing
30. Lucky Seven
31. Bim Bam Records
32. Allen
33. Gaz's Rockin' Blues
34. La Trolley Bergere
35. Garageman
36. Mama Con Yuca
37. Johnny Hoodoo
38. Sonic Friction
39. Entertainer
40. Brat Pack
41. The Count
42. Rock-Olla-Eddy
43. Ant Aktion

Plus Wheelie Bags where numbers appear to be missing or up the creek:

Debbie Does Mk 2
Show Box
Radio Wheelie Bag
Maria Maraca
Orange Spot
Bootlegger

50. Wheelie Bag Mk4

WHEELIE BAG PRICE AND DELIVERY

I charge £50 a day to design and make each Wheelie Bag and they take me from about 5-6 days to complete. To this must be added the cost of materials and equipment. This depends a bit on the Pound–Euro as most of the parts come from Europe.

The active speaker will cost around £150 – for 70w and £200 – for 100w. The deck will cost around £100 and the mixer £75.

The box is constructed from sheet polycarbonate and will cost about £100 the adhesive vinyl covering a further £75. Lights, fittings and wheels will be about £100.

So altogether the total cost of the parts that make up each Sound Machine is at least £600.

Any special effects such as animated movements, fading or flashing lights, glitter balls etc are all possible but will be additional to the above.

UK buyers collect from central London. Delivery in Europe is about £147 (door to door with Easy Sending.com).